EXPLORING WORLD CULTURES

Chile

Alicia Z. Klepeis

Cavendish
Square

New York

Published in 2020 by Cavendish Square Publishing, LLC
243 5th Avenue, Suite 136, New York, NY 10016

Copyright © 2020 by Cavendish Square Publishing, LLC

First Edition

Library of Congress Cataloging-in-Publication Data

Names: Klepeis, Alicia, 1971- author.
Title: Chile / Alicia Z. Klepeis.
Description: First edition. | New York : Cavendish Square, 2020. |
Series: Exploring world cultures | Includes index.
Identifiers: LCCN 2018044399 (print) | LCCN 2018046526 (ebook) |
ISBN 9781502647092 (ebook) | ISBN 9781502647085 (library bound) |
ISBN 9781502647061 (pbk.) | ISBN 9781502647078 (6 pack)
Subjects: LCSH: Chile--Juvenile literature.
Classification: LCC F3058.5 (ebook) | LCC F3058.5 .K54 2020 (print) | DDC 983--dc23
LC record available at https://lccn.loc.gov/2018044399

Editorial Director: David McNamara
Editor: Lauren Miller
Copy Editor: Nathan Heidelberger
Associate Art Director: Alan Sliwinski
Designer: Christina Shults
Production Coordinator: Karol Szymczuk
Photo Research: J8 Media

Contents

Introduction

Chile is a country in South America. People have lived in Chile for thousands of years. Different groups have ruled what is now Chile during its history. Today, Chile is a free country. Its government is a **democracy**.

People in Chile have many kinds of jobs. Some work in banks or schools. Others have jobs in stores, hospitals, or offices. Chileans also work in mines and factories.

Chile has lots of beautiful places to visit. There are deserts, beaches, and mountains. Tourists come from around the world to see the country's national parks and historic cities.

The Chilean people have many traditions. They value the arts. Dancing is popular here. Chile's nickname is the Land of Poets. Chileans also enjoy playing sports like soccer and eating good food. Festivals and celebrations take place all year long.

Chile is a fascinating country to explore.

Torres del Paine National Park, located in a region called Patagonia, is known for its beautiful landscapes.

Geography

Chile sits on South America's western coast. It is a long, narrow country. The Pacific Ocean lies to the west. Three other countries border Chile. They are Argentina, Bolivia, and Peru. The country covers 291,933 square miles (756,102 square kilometers).

This map shows Chile and its neighbors.

The deserts in northern Chile are very dry. Southern Chile, on the other hand, is cool and damp.

Chile's Plants and Animals

Chile has many plants and animals. Plants like cacti, ferns, and flowers grow here. Unique animals like alpacas, flamingos, and even penguins live here too.

Alpacas can be found in Lauca National Park.

The Andes Mountains run down Chile's eastern side. The highest point is Nevado Ojos del Salado. It is 22,572 feet (6,880 meters) tall. A huge valley sits in central Chile. You can find many farms here.

The Atacama Desert spreads across northern Chile. It is one of the driest places on Earth!

People have lived in what is now Chile for a long time. In fact, **prehistoric** people lived here.

The Plaza de Armas has been the center of Santiago since 1541.

A group called the Inca once ruled northern Chile. These American Indian people farmed and built roads. The roads connected their cities. The Mapuche people, another native group, lived in central and southern Chile.

FACT!

In 2010, a huge earthquake hit central Chile. Hundreds of people died.

In the 1530s, Spanish explorers first came to Chile. They built the city of Santiago in 1541. They fought with the groups living there and won. Spain ruled Chile until the early 1800s. In 1818, Chile became an independent country.

Chile's most famous leader was a **dictator** named Augusto Pinochet. He ruled Chile from 1973 to 1990. The country returned to a democracy in 1990. Chile's government is strong today.

A portrait of Bernardo O'Higgins.

Bernardo O'Higgins

Bernardo O'Higgins fought for Chile's independence. He also founded libraries, hospitals, and colleges during the 1800s.

Chile is a democracy. It has sixteen regions. The capital of Chile is Santiago. The government's buildings and workers are in the city of Valparaíso.

The National Congress Building in Valparaíso.

Chile's government has three parts, legislative, judicial, and executive. The legislative part is called the National Congress. Members of the National Congress write new laws. Chile's National Congress has two parts, or

FACT!

All Chilean citizens over the age of eighteen can vote in elections.

Michelle Bachelet

Chile's first female president was Michelle Bachelet. She led the country from 2006 to 2010, and from 2014 to 2018.

Michelle Bachelet was the president of Chile.

houses. They are the Senate and the Chamber of Deputies. As of 2018, the Senate had 43 members. The Chamber of Deputies had 155 members.

The judicial part is made up of courts. They follow the country's constitution. The constitution describes all the basic laws of Chile. It was adopted in 1980. The executive part includes the president and the cabinet of advisors. The president runs the government.

The Economy

Chile has one of the largest **economies** in South America. Chile trades with countries like China, the United States, and Brazil. The country's money is called the Chilean peso.

A factory worker packs socks that are made with copper thread.

Many people in Chile work to help others. Some work in restaurants, hotels, and banks. Others have jobs in schools, stores, and hospitals. Some people help tourists when they visit the country.

More than six million tourists visited Chile from other countries in 2017.

Chile and Copper

Chile is the world's biggest producer of copper. Copper is used in products such as wires, pipes, and coins.

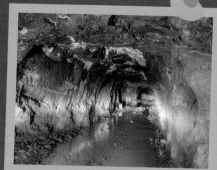

The entrance to a copper and gold mine.

Factories in Chile make many different items. Some make common things, like cloth and cement. Others make food or drinks, like canned fish and wine.

Farmers grow crops including grapes, apples, and wheat. Fishermen work on Chile's coast. Workers called miners dig for gemstones and minerals like copper.

Chile has many unique plants and animals. Alpacas and chinchillas live in the mountains. Pumas, pudu deer, and llamas live in forests and the plains of central Chile. Flamingos, penguins, and sea lions live along the coast.

Chinchillas have thick fur that keeps them warm in the Andes Mountains.

The monkey puzzle tree, or Chile pine, is the national tree. It is found in the Valdivian forests of

FACT!

The Andean cat and the short-tailed chinchilla are two rare animals living in Chile.

14

southern Chile. These trees are some of the oldest in the world. Unfortunately, many are being cut down for business.

The capital of Santiago can be covered by smog.

Air pollution is also a problem. It comes from cars, factories, and firewood used to heat homes. Electric and gas heaters are becoming more common. They are cleaner than fireplaces.

Clean Energy in Chile

Chile gets about 30 percent of its electricity from water power. Another 16 percent comes from other **renewable** sources like the sun or the wind.

Nearly eighteen million people live in Chile. It is home to several different **ethnic groups**. Almost nine out of ten people here are white or a mixture of European and American Indian.

These statues called *moai* were made by the Rapa Nui.

Chile's second-largest group is the Mapuche people. They make up about 9 percent of Chileans. In the past, the Mapuche

FACT!

The average Chilean has a life expectancy of 78.9 years.

The Rapa Nui People

The Rapa Nui are people of **Polynesian** heritage. They live on Easter Island. It is off Chile's coast. The Rapa Nui are known for their huge statues.

were farmers. Today, some Mapuche sell crafts or are involved in tourism. Many Mapuche live in the south-central part of Chile.

The Aymara are the third-largest group in Chile. They make up about 0.7 percent of the population. Today, most Aymara people live and work in the coastal cities of Iquique and Arica. However, some also live in northern Chile's high plains. There, they herd llamas and sheep. They also grow potatoes and barley.

Lifestyle

In Chile, over 87 percent of the population lives in cities or towns. Some live in apartments. Others live in houses. People in the city might take a train or bus to work, or ride a bike.

Many people living in Santiago use the public bus system.

City residents often have cell phones and use computers. Many own cars too.

Others live in crowded areas outside cities. These areas are called *callampas* (ka-YAM-pas).

Most Chilean families have one or two children.

Homes there are small. Many people living there do not have electricity or running water.

In Chile's countryside, people work on farms or in mines. Along the coast, some Chileans work in the fishing industry. Most people in the countryside live in traditional houses made of a clay mixture called adobe.

Women in the Workforce

Almost half of people working in Chile are women. Most work in service jobs. Traditional jobs for women are teachers, nurses, or helpers around the home. However, Chilean women are becoming doctors, judges, and more.

A worker harvests grapes at the Casa Silva vineyard.

Religion

Religion is important for many Chileans. In Chile, people can practice whatever religion they want. Most people are Christian. Many are Roman Catholic

A statue of the Virgen del Carmen is carried during a festival.

Christians. About 16 percent of Chile's people are Protestant or Evangelical.

Chilean Christians celebrate holidays such as Christmas and Easter. They also have festivals

More than 11 percent of Chileans do not follow a religion.

Churches of Chiloé

Off the coast of Chile, the Chiloé **archipelago** is home to about seventy wooden churches. These churches have unique designs and bright colors.

One of the colorful wooden churches found in Chiloé.

for Catholic saints during the year. These festivals sometimes include carrying religious statues through the streets.

Some Chileans believe in other religions. The Mapuche have their own religious beliefs and traditions. *Machi* are Mapuche spiritual healers. People believe the *machi* communicate with spirits or gods.

21

Language

Nearly everyone in Chile speaks Spanish. Spanish is the official language of Chile. The government uses Spanish. Children are also taught in Spanish in Chile's schools. Many people speak Spanish for business matters.

At Santiago's international airport, signs are written in Spanish and English.

FACT!

About twenty-one thousand people in Chile speak Chilean sign language.

Some Chileans speak more than one language. Many ethnic groups have their own languages. Many Mapuche people speak Mapudungun. Other native languages include Aymara, Quechua, and Rapa Nui.

About 10 percent of Chileans speak English. Chile's Ministry of Education wants to raise that number. It has a program called English Opens Doors. The goal is to make sure that every Chilean student receives one thousand hours of English learning during school.

Arts and Festivals

The Chilean people enjoy many kinds of art. Painting and sculpture are common. The native peoples of Chile create beautiful weavings and handmade baskets.

Dancers perform the cueca on Independence Day.

Dancing is an important part of Chilean culture. The cueca is Chile's national dance. Women perform in colorful clothes. Men dress as cowboys.

Chilean music has many styles. Pop, jazz, and folk music are popular. A traditional instrument

featured in Chilean music is the charango. It is shaped like a guitar but has ten strings.

Chileans enjoy festivals all year round. They celebrate Independence Day on September 18. On this day, there are parades and horse races. Children fly kites and play with spinning tops and marbles.

Gabriela Mistral

Gabriela Mistral was a famous Chilean poet. She won the Nobel Prize in Literature in 1945.

There are many ways to have fun in Chile. Soccer is the biggest sport here. The national soccer team is the most popular. They are known for having red jerseys.

A hiker admires the mountains of Patagonia.

Chile's national sport is rodeo. Rodeos came from the tradition of cowboys rounding up cattle.

Tourists and Chileans like to hike. Patagonia is a popular area to explore. This region includes

FACT!

People from around the world come to the Andes Mountains to ski and snowboard.

Sandboarding in the Atacama Desert

The Atacama Desert is the perfect place to sandboard. People use snowboards to sail over the sand dunes. Some dunes are 400 feet (120 m) tall!

The Caraucho Dunes are a popular spot for sandboarding.

the Andes Mountains, grasslands, and deserts. Along the coast, Chileans like to sail and surf.

One unusual Chilean game is *palo encebado* (PAH-lo en-say-BAH-doh). Players try to climb a 16-foot (5 m) log that's greased or covered in soap. Prizes are hung at the top of the log!

Food

People in Chile eat lots of different foods. Corn and potatoes are popular ingredients in Chilean cooking. *Humitas* (oo-ME-tas) are a quick meal. They

This Chilean fruit is called a cherimoya.

are made of mashed corn that is wrapped in corn husks and cooked.

Seafood like conger eel is popular. It can be made into a soup with onions and potatoes.

FACT!

Coffee and fruit juices are among the most popular drinks in Chile.

A Sweet Treat

Manjar is a Chilean treat. It's a sweet caramel-like spread made from condensed milk and sugar. People often eat it on bread for breakfast.

Chileans often eat stews called *cazuelas* (cah-ZWAY-lahs). They typically contain meat, vegetables, and noodles or rice.

When the weather is warm, people in Chile like to grill. An *asado* (ah-SAH-doh) is a Chilean barbeque. Chileans grill steak, sausages, and ribs.

Many fruits are available in Chile. Grapes, avocadoes, apples, and peaches grow here.

Glossary

archipelago A group of islands.

democracy A system of government in which leaders are chosen by the people.

dictator A person who rules with complete authority, often in a cruel manner.

economy The use of money and goods in a country.

ethnic groups Groups of people who share a common culture or ancestry.

Polynesian People from the Polynesian Islands in the Pacific Ocean.

prehistoric The time before written history.

renewable Referring to a source of energy that does not run out when used.

Find Out More

Books

Burgan, Michael. *Chile*. Enchantment of the World.
New York: Children's Press, 2016.

Morrison, Marion. *Chile*. Countries Around the World.
North Mankato, MN: Heinemann-Raintree, 2012.

Website

Chile

https://kids.nationalgeographic.com/explore/
countries/chile

Video

The Essence of Chile

http://www.natgeotraveller.co.uk/photography-video/
video-of-the-week/travel-video-week-chile
A video of Chile's many beautiful landscapes.

Index

About the Author

Alicia Z. Klepeis began her career at the National Geographic Society. She is the author of many kids' books, including *Snakes Are Awesome*, *The World's Strangest Foods*, and *A Time for Change*. Klepeis lives with her family in upstate New York.